MW01130432

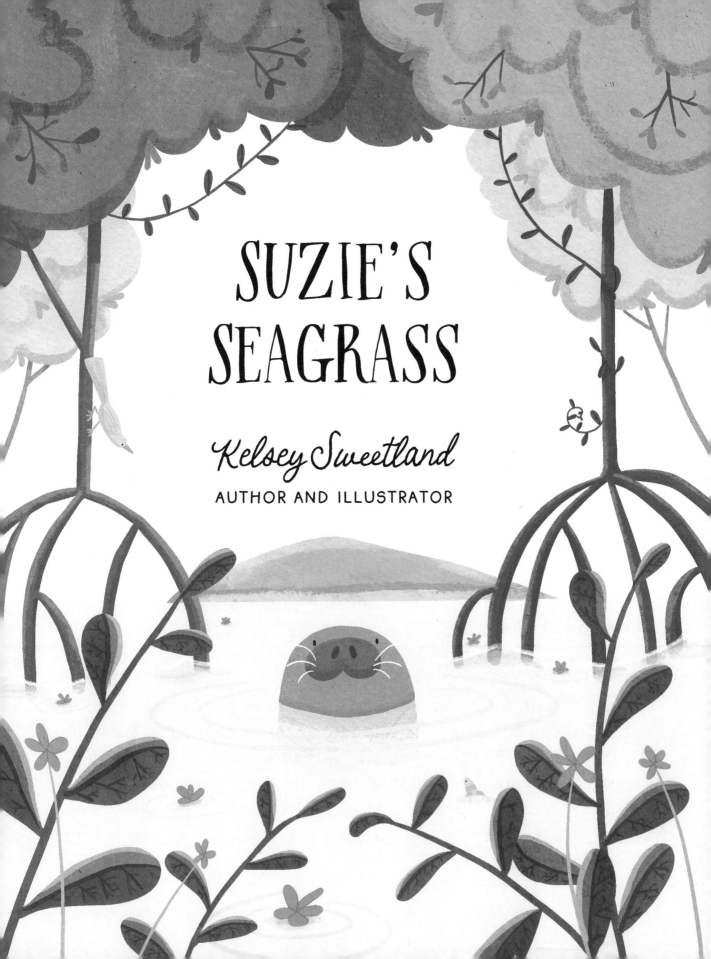

SUZIE'S SEAGRASS

Kelsey Sweetland

AUTHOR AND ILLUSTRATOR

⁒ Save the Manatees! ⁒

Manatees, also known as sea cows, are curious, intelligent, and adorable creatures that live in tropical areas around the world. Their main source of food is seagrass, and they travel between salt and fresh water to find food and shelter. Manatees love to perform barrel rolls underwater, body surf to amuse themselves, and are even known to curiously swim up to kayakers! Unfortunately, these playful creatures are very vulnerable to human activity. Manatees are often hit by boats and are facing massive food shortages due to severe water pollution, which kills their main source of food, seagrass.

In 2021, The Florida Fish and Wildlife Conservation Commission (FFWCC) found that one out of every four adult manatees showed evidence of ten or more watercraft strikes and that only 4% of all adult manatees had no watercraft-related scars! This shows how frequently manatees are hit by boats. These watercraft strikes can permanently harm manatees' fins and bones, and they can even be deadly to these playful creatures.

Although 20 - 25% of all manatee deaths are caused by watercraft impact (FFWCC), possibly the most pressing issue Manatees face is starvation due to seagrass shortages. The journal, Proceedings of the National Academy of Sciences estimated that at least 29% of the known seagrass in the world has disappeared in the last 200 years and that the rate of disappearance is continuing to accelerate. PNAS also explained that the rate we are losing seagrass is comparable to that of mangroves, coral reefs, and tropical forests, which makes seagrass meadows some of the most threatened ecosystems on the planet.

Seagrass exists all over the globe, and it faces different challenges depending on its location. The main issue Florida seagrass faces is water pollution. Seagrass needs direct sunlight and clean water to stay healthy, and when the water becomes polluted, it can lead to massive seagrass die-offs, which causes manatees to starve. For example, the Indian River Lagoon, one of the most important habitats for the Florida manatee, has been facing massive seagrass die-offs due to septic tank leakage and fertilizers clouding the water in the lagoon. According to Charles Jacoby, supervising environmental scientist for the St. Johns River Water Management District, from 2009 to 2021, the Indian River Lagoon lost at least 58% of its seagrass, and the Banana River, a connecting river to the lagoon, lost at least 96%! This decline in seagrass, combined with harmful algae blooms that cause massive seagrass die-offs, has led to manatees starving to death at unprecedented rates.

Not only is seagrass important to manatees, but it is also important to many other creatures, such as the green sea turtle, sharks, fish, crabs, and different species of octopi. Seagrass is also incredibly important for absorbing CO_2 out of the atmosphere. Per the World Wildlife Foundation, seagrass captures up to 35% more CO_2 than tropical rainforests, and although seagrass only covers 0.2% of the seafloor, it absorbs 10% of the ocean's carbon every year! Seagrass often grows in mangrove forests which are also important habitats for manatees to feed and raise their young. By protecting seagrass and mangroves, we would not only be protecting manatees' main food source but also an important habitat for many creatures.

Luckily, it is not too late to change our ways, and there are many things we can do to help! Here are a few suggestions:

- If you live near manatees, plant seagrass, drive boats safely, pick up trash, regularly check septic tanks for leaks, and reduce the amount of fertilizer you use, especially before it rains.
- If you do not live in an area near manatees, you can help by donating to nonprofits like WWF, Save the Manatee, Center for Biological Diversity, and Project Seagrass.
- And last but definitely not least, spread awareness about this issue. We need more people to know about the problems manatees face, so they can get more help and support.

Thank you for spending time reading about manatees and the issues they currently face. These gentle giants are one of the many species that are directly affected by negative human activity, and we need more people to know about what is happening to our earth and its animals to better protect them. Luckily, we have time to change our ways and make sure that manatees have the safe, happy, seagrass-filled life they deserve.

⋛ Dedication ⋚

To all the children reading this book and
the hope you give to the future

Down in the warm Florida rivers
lives a manatee named SUZIE.

Suzie lives with her mom and her curious twin brother, Samuel. They love to swim in rivers, bays, and marshy coasts, and their very favorite thing to do is eat their favorite food... SEAGRASS.

A few years ago, all their favorite rivers and bays were filled with healthy SEAGRASS, but one day, the seagrass started to die.

That morning, the MANATEES woke up bright and early to look for their seagrass breakfast, but as they searched, they discovered that all the seagrass in the river was gone! Suzie and her family decided they must find new SEAGRASS, so they set off and began to search.

First, they swam to a large winding RIVER.

SUZIE looked near the riverbank and saw many ferns and bright FLOWERS.

Next, she swam around the river bend. Suddenly a bunch of quick colorful FISH darted past, but there was no seagrass in sight.

No matter how hard they looked, Suzie and her family couldn't find any seagrass in the RIVER.

Next, they decided to search the big blue BAY.

SUZIE swam over to a steep rocky CLIFF with many large colorful plants, but she couldn't find any seagrass there.

As they searched, a loud BOAT suddenly zoomed overhead. They quickly swam deep underwater, and after the roaring faded, they continued to look for their seagrass.

Suzie's family searched the entire BAY, but there was no seagrass anywhere!

Next, they decided to explore a MANGROVE FOREST.

As Suzie searched, she found fish, coral, and crabs around the long MANGROVE roots.

Suzie then heard a noise and looked out of the water to find a GREAT BLUE HERON catching fish for lunch. But no matter how hard they searched the mangrove forest, they couldn't find any seagrass.

Suzie and her family were swimming out to the big blue BAY when suddenly the sky turned dark. They curiously looked out of the water and saw a massive STORM heading their way!

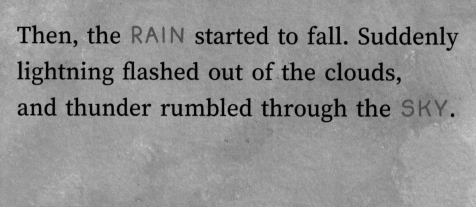

Then, the RAIN started to fall. Suddenly lightning flashed out of the clouds, and thunder rumbled through the SKY.

They looked around and quickly found
a nearby RIVER. Suzie and her family swam
upstream to escape the crashing ocean WAVES,
and for the rest of the night, the manatees slept
in the river's gentle current and waited for the big
STORM to pass.

When they woke up the next MORNING, the storm had ended, and the sky was clear again.

Suzie and her family looked around at the new RIVER. They noticed that the water was crystal clear, no boats were zooming over them, and the plants looked healthy. They swam a bit further upstream, and then, they suddenly FOUND...

SEAGRASS! It was waving in the gentle
river current and looked healthy and delicious!

Suzie and her family finally feasted on SEAGRASS and decided to stay in the beautiful new river.

Then, the DAY was over,

the SUN set,

and the SKY turned dark.

SUZIE and her family all fell asleep with full stomachs and beautiful memories of their exciting ADVENTURE.